The Aging Cheerleader's Alphabet

Jeanette Lynes

THE AGING CHEERLEADER'S ALPHABET

Mansfield Press

National Library of Canada Cataloguing in Publication

Lynes, Jeanette
    The aging cheerleaders alphabet / Jeanette Lynes.

Poems.
ISBN 1-894469-15-1

    I. Title.

PS8573.Y6A76 2003   C811'.54   C2003-905350-4

Cover Design: *Angela Gulia & Denis De Klerck*
Text Design: *Denis De Klerck*
Technical Advisor: *Tim Hanna*
Author Photo: *Bernice MacDonald*
Cover Painting, CROWN OF WEEDS: *Gillian McCulloch*

THE CANADA COUNCIL | LE CONSEIL DES ARTS
FOR THE ARTS | DU CANADA
SINCE 1957 | DEPUIS 1957

The publication of
The Aging Cheerleader's Alphabet
has been generously supported by
The Canada Council for the Arts and
The Ontario Arts Council.

ONTARIO ARTS COUNCIL
CONSEIL DES ARTS DE L'ONTARIO

Mansfield Press Inc.
25 MANSFIELD AVENUE, TORONTO, ONTARIO, CANADA. M6J 2A9
Publisher: *Denis De Klerck*
www.mansfieldpress.net

For my sister-in-laws:
Beth, Cecile, Claudia, Evy, Katie
and
for my godson, Jonathan

Contents

The Aging Cheerleader's Alphabet

III   The Flames

IV   Prologue

"Blister, wizen. It's worth it and it's night.
Who wants pretty, when pretty is plain
and the heart is gnarled and the fullsacked
forest of being lost is home?"

Brenda Shaughnessy,
"Voluptuary"

"Return in thought to the concert where music flared.
You gathered acorns in the park in autumn
and leaves eddied over the earth's scars.
Praise the mutilated world
and the gray feathers a thrush lost,
and the gentle light that strays and vanishes
and returns."

Adam Zagajewski,
"Try to Praise the Mutilated World"

I
EPILOGUE

EPILOGUE

I'm too young for an epilogue. But the team wants a Memory Book.
Does every song begin with capitulation?

I only hope
it's not over. Epilogue,
I'll rebut you –

Some say I've laid down
my poms for good. Bosh. Even now, they dreadlock my sofa,
two shaggy pillows playing at sleep. I still keep

a hand in it – why? – because the world needs cheering, home team
craves The Wave, sometimes home team
is only you. Even in my La-Z-Boy, I tell myself, in affectionate tones,
lift those arms, raise them high.

A stadium united
in fervor still gives me that shiver. Quiver the same as when,
in bag-lady disguise I wander the hippodrome before the game,
watch them paint the lines.
When Security asks can they help me, I say *Go, Flames, win & burn!*
Oh, Flames, soar & turn! (their cue to
escort me out).

Sometimes home team suffers a slump, a legend-warped
smack in the face. Take me. Why remember the fallen, why not
triumph, first six-high pyramid (though yes, a long
way down).

This fall yields such lush, such longing to be
in the game, I wail like a quarterback with tied ankles.

The cheerleader cheers, but who cheers for the cheerleader?
Who listens
while aloud I read (in animated tones)
from Browning's "Epilogue to Asolando" –
Greet the unseen with a cheer!

II
JURASSIC SKIN

AUDITION

"If you're from Texas and one day you get chosen to be a Cowboys Cheerleader, it's right up there with your wedding day. And depending on who you marry, it might even be bigger."

— Suzette Scholz, Former Dallas Cowboys Cheerleader

We all take sides some time. They said I used my body, those bitter raisins
                                                        who couldn't
make the cut. Of course I did. Fifth of Wild Turkey in the coach's
El Camino didn't hurt, either. I sang *I am Woman, Hear me Roar*
in both official languages. The Executive Flames said I'd fire on my tongue.

I became a Cinderette. I'd wanted that since before birth, I suppose.
Mother said I did handsprings in Lake Amniotic.

I'll take twenty shares in Hope, Inc. Oh, I've seen
the other side, was only a go-go girl in love with someone
who didn't care. I pulled myself up by my pom poms. Sartre said
the world is what you make it. I'm worth all the Pepnocrats put together.
Yes I am. I used

my body, so sue me, what else is there? With my throat
behind them, The Flames couldn't lose. Such days, whole falls I didn't
touch earth. I was part prayer, part cabaret. I can still out-tumble you
old sour grapes who snub me in the grocery aisles. A pep queen never
forgets. You think falling was easy? Let me remind you
fire is never entirely wholesome.

ENIGMA IN RED & WHITE

I wear my old uniform to the supermarket, big white
fuzzy F on my chest. I'm no dull shopper; catching air,
my red pleats still burst into plucky blooms as I drop,
doing splits, to the bottom shelf (instant pie filling).
Everyone else wears a uniform, too –
blue blue blue denim denim. *What's the F
for?* someone always asks. *Food*, I say, *nutrition
for the spirit.* Or they'll want to know where
the game is. Did I tell you my lip curls
like Mona Lisa's?[1] I do that enigmatic thing with my mouth –
there's always a game somewhere, I say.

That shuts them up. If you *must* ripen, learn to speak in riddles.

[1] The more astute among you will have noticed
that Leonardo's great painting lacks any real
background. I have it on good authority that
Mona was at market mulling over snails, mak-
ing her final selection for escargot – only snails
could make a woman smile that way, non?

WHAT IS IT YOU DO?

Let me begin with Greek lyric poetry. Pindar's *Olympian Odes*
wherein we are told: *I have many swift arrows in my quiver*
which speak to the wise, but for the crowd

they need interpreters. The skilled poet who has learned her art
chatters turbulently, like a raven, vainly, against the divine
bird of Zeus. OK Pindar didn't say

her, but go with me here. Please. Thank you.
If each game's a lyric poem, the cheerleader's the raven, winging down
praise, vainly

or not. To not place too fine a point on it, one can't climb Olympus
then say *no comment.* The world would be filled
with turbulent chatter, tough job someone

must do, though the field be slicked with mud (have you
ever been privy to the smell of trampled grass
in fall?). What of *vainly,* you ask? Shift from Pindar

to Keats. I mean devotion amid uncertainties, dashed hopes.
I mean negative jumpability, great dazzlements of poms, doing The Wave
'til your elbows ache, 'til the muse is bruised

from trying. No one said squaring off against the big bird (Zeus)
would be a snap. We bleed for our craft, suffer
for art – but we are *not* dominatrixes on our days off!

BULLHORN

1. Preparation. I don my parade gloves like the poet, before open
stanza surgery, washes her hands & applies a good
moisturizing soap. No one likes dry poems.

2. Inspiration. I invoke the muse – my mother
who rose through adversity to become Twirling Champ of '48. I place
beside me some beloved volume – Humphreys, Syzmborska, McKay.

3. Or lowbrow inspiration. I play *Abba Gold*, reminds me of the cosmic
potential for harmony.

4. Selection. There are three basic pom clasps – cap handle, bike grip,
show handle. Consider that fingers have throats. They must be cleared.
What poet would write with a squeaky HP pencil? Without a
glassful of quills to choose from?

5. The Pom Itself. Shake it new –
These just in: wet-look wide-strand dance pom;
            pre-fluffed vinyl pom with metallic sparkle option;
            single-strand streamer show pom;
            space-age all-metallic pom with two-toned target pattern
            & two-hundred strand count.
What artist would sleep
on anything under two-hundred thread count?

6. Amplification. (Being ready to begin. By now, an unmistakable nip
has crept in, dusk impends) –
this is where bullhorn
                  becomes page, where, when
we're certain the world couldn't care
less, we
                  raise a lettered hand, say *yes.*

FACE

Mirror, mirror. Houston, we've got a problem. Lines of scrimmage.
Miss Havisham trying to get out. What to do.

I remember an Oil of Olay ad – Joe Student, for the first time sees
the glow, the staggering vitality of
his English teacher. It won't happen. The boy I teach twirling
every other Saturday doesn't even
notice me.

I imagine myself a grand old warrior. Like Barbara Ann Scott,
World Figure Skating Champ of '48, tuck-edged eyes still scanning
the cold rink for that spot of light.
                    It's not there.

My face knows its niche – wicked queen in Disney's next flick.
Beauty snuffed by a wayward soul.

STUDY

Sedum reddens under my window
as I sleep, spins its crimmy mauve bumbershoots. The scholars
come & go, talking of vertigo, subcultures.
Hegemony? – Goodness no, I haven't trimmed my own hedge in years.
The aging quarterback serves me well in *that* quarter.

Doctor Sally pins a wire to my
sweater, says –
You're the last living member of your squad –
just talk.

               (Surely being the last living *anything*

warrants a *please?*) I feel like Charlton Heston, final scene,
The Planet of the Apes.
The last Dionne quintuplet, beleaguered, still, by flashbulbs.

Why do they never stroll through my air gallery of cable-free stunts
or ask, do I grieve? Why not suppose *my* heart, too, has lain
tackled, splayed all over
the end zone?

I AM INVITED TO WOMEN'S STUDIES CLASS

Not their politics that faze me, their peach-yogurt skin.
I might as well be Mrs. Robinson in a room of Elaines.

How did it feel, being bauble,
                    accessory to patriarchy?

Might I have a glass
of water, please?

How could you sleep, demoted to air
                    head, sex toy,
                    no more than
                    an exotic dancer?

That came later, Winnipeg. Before that, my art was pure, all moves
connected –   flier to base,
                    scorpion to liberty,
                    banana to basket toss.

Could you be deluded? Surely you can't deny being a contemporary
of Barbie?

My glass empty. Led out, an Elaine squeezes my hand, whispers:
I always wanted the camper. And Ken.

WHAT THE NEIGHBOURS THINK

I'm one of those crocheted poodles slid
over the Kleenex box. A cliché. Aggregate of cosmetics.
I can tell by how they hold the elevator door
open for me. They think I turn tricks for
the big win, biscuit of approval. They think I'm
a freak show & they're
a nice family.

Christ on a cracker it's good
they've gone. Things are looking up. I live beside an *artiste*, now,
a stand-up comic. I press my glass to the wall, hear Ms. Ham
run through her routines. Listen while the funny woman
cries, blows her nose. For once a spade's a spade, things are real –
the comic doesn't wear a mask,
she *is* a mask.

CALLERS

Ever had a day of rare convergences?
A painterly day
that struck you dumb? Prussian sky braided with lapis, earth all sorrel,
celadon, cerise, saffron. Creamy mounds
of puce-tipped hydrangea. A day you kick yourself for leaving
art school. Still, to dab patchouli on your throat, to stand, arranging fudge
on your good crystal plate, watching the yard fill with crows
is enough. The sky's roped with white, puffy twine, dark bird there – there –
there. A day that invites: *ride the bumper car of conviction & make sure*
you've clean bobby socks on, in case of an accident, just as
your mother said. Today there's nothing you wouldn't praise. It's just as
your mother advised: *a genial soul attracts many* (& couldn't *she* fly?).
So the knocking at the gate
doesn't surprise you.

It's the harlequinade from next door. She's soon up to her funny
bones in fudge. Then crunching (you both hear) through dried lily stalks,
the manly knock, massive shoulder pads, gust of redolent jock strap,
the old quarterback
blows in, is happy
to come in
out of it, the day's onrush of peerless mauve light, its astoundment.

DATE

I told him the landfill site wasn't my idea of
a romantic outing. But what else was there

to do? So we set off for Mount Bentmetal, his trunk
stuffed with yard refuse (he'd kill two birds

with one stone). We wound our way past
Appliance Foothills, a butte of retired

bread machines, bikes, bikes (tossed in that
reckless way we did, summers, adash through

some screen door, a waiting pitcher of Kool-Aid).
We entered the Highlands of Ash, the ancient

tribes of obsolescence, dead wringers, old wire
cages trapped in fires, lost

fight songs eaten at
from the inside.

MONUMENT PARK

"When you see a bust of ancient, broken personage, someone
without a name is running faster."

Brenda Shaughnessy, *"Musée"*

A leaf chitters down, lands
on my shoulder. Why that leaf,
this shoulder? Does the brittle little biocourier
seek *me*, or is it simply the old
one-armed bandit in Casino Universe
in play again? Another leaf, other shoulder. I'm going to take this

personally. So – despite the random rhythms of the cosmos
someone, at least, has a sense of symmetry. Perhaps if I remain
in these conquered shadows, if I'm very, very still, I'll be taken
for a woman in a myth, the one

whose fingers sprouted boughs. Taken as once splendid, now ruined
arboretum.

The children, well-schooled in hazard, paddle in maple pools,
avoiding me. *Don't talk to strangers*, written all over their body
language, clearly extends to aging cheerleaders. To tender
eyes, I'm only another

more dangerous monument. *Kids, kids*, I'd like to say. *It's ok –*
I'm completely, completely biodegradable.

THE POETICS OF CELESTIAL FATIGUE

Angels have tired mouths, Rilke said.

Oh, I know, I know. Though the poet
might be faulted for failing to extend his
analogy to the long line of twirlers, heart lifters, spirit rousers
here on earth. Rilke was a gloomy man who never
led a pep rally. A melancholy soul consumed by death.

My mouth is tired.

There are too many unfinished thoughts (poetry).
(Life) too replete with the unappreciated.

Old football injuries get broken
into noble beats, the finger food of myth – but lines
around a worn mouth?
                    Who praises them?

Any poem is an unequal playing yield (like heaven).

AMONG THE BOOKS

I'm signing out Sappho. The librarian
wears, dangling, a comet-sized watch. You must be
very aware of time, I say. She only keeps sliding books

over a glass-lidded casket. I walk out. Blue jays have gutted the sun
flowers, mist abounds. Alumni mist, swamped
in its own sageness.

If I were not carrying Sappho, I might say this day
has been simmering in a crockpot
so long, it would crumble if stirred with a lyrical spoon. It dares you

to have feelings. I'll leave that to the Greek lady bard. Sappho
your poems are an ancient
lump of peat. In my palm. Smoldering.

Frost gnawed my earlobes (Great Game of '71).
Lend me your thaw. It grows dark. I must dash home, read you.
The path frazzled by puce

aster heads, ambushed by rime. I could kick them,
those Michaelmas daisies, for
such a poor affray.

SCAPE

"All forms of landscape are autobiographical."

Charles Wright

I wish, just once, to see
myself in the fringed, derelict hills. To commiserate with
the blasted tree – *I've been there, you poor old bark; I've peered
at the world through ancient, cracking mascara.*
                    I'd like the clump of ruined grass to say
my name, chronicle

my moulting poms
& wouldn't I weep if the ablaze   passionate sumach
matched my red sweater?
If the sticks El Stormo puffed about were silver, I'd envision
my mother – Twirling Queen of '48 –

instead of just sticks. Unjust sticks – perhaps I am
posthumous –
                    nothing out there
contradicts.

I IMAGINE HEAVEN

Bigger than Costco, whole wing
devoted to cheerleaders.

To decide if it's time
Management meets over lunch
(angel food cake).

I'm up.

Let's get this over with – what about her? –
Thumbs up ____ or: down ____?

It's a draw. They call the celestial coach.

(This line, a higher caucus) –

All right, give her this one,
allow a body
for another day:

(a great sending up of balloons)

I IMAGINE NORTH

Run but can't
hide. Even most
epic rivers
mere ribbons,
vanish in a
single yank
under their
own ice.

Each animal
an exposed flash
bulb bang in the quick
press of light.
Collared lemming
chomps lichen, what
turns out his last
supper.

Hunters and
more hunters.
Someone always
loses, it's all
niche markets.

Then there's
humans, the harm
they do with willow
twigs, sprigs of
copper. *A harm*
say the scholars behind
their tagged heaps
of ribs & snagged
ancient hair
sent special
delivery to the heart.

IMAGE

Look inward, angel. Clear your head. Drive north.
It worked – when I came out the other side, my noggin was completely
empty. Where's my head at? I bought a home x-ray kit, placed said head
under it. It resembled a VCR, the machine, I mean. Tracking, tracking,
bingo – my cerebrum's beautiful, not rumpled, not crimped to shreds
like those gross brains in medical texts, but smooth to a fault,
bottle shaped. There's me, dressed in long trailing scrims, some kind
of headdress. Lounging on a sofa. Listen. I'm saying *yes, master*.
What's this shit? I saw this on TV once. Maybe
my old squad leader was right, you are what you watch.

AMONG THE MOUNTIES

Stunned by the vigour a northern
sun can have, we zoom our lenses
straight up, shoot the heat, the shimmy
shimmy shoo shoo air.

I make sense here. The Chateau Laurier (dear
old biddy) allows my face, winnowed
with lancet traceries, pinnacled with crockets in the optic area

to fit in – I arrive at a deeper architectural knowledge
of myself – I'm Gothic Revival! (at last
a way to explain the ruining eye that kidnapped

me). Then there's the musical ride – have you ever seen anything more
charming in your life? They thread the needle with four
now eight now
twelve horses, never drop a stitch. Oh can I
die happy, now. Among the Mounties
I'm at one with the cosmos, not to mention
safe as hell.

REVISION

I thought I was safe. But sometimes, the Loneliness All-Stars
snatch my heels, tug with such
harrowing ardour, I backflip through time, land in 1977, a day
I know well – champion of autumn afternoons. If there was
an Autumnal Hall of Fame, this day would
hang there. The streets, I recognize the streets! (lined with coral
leaves aflame) – the dappled light, the sweet nose-punch of popcorn butter,
it's game day &

lord, my *face* – ultra-suede smooth, tanned. My hair
its real colour. Ragtops down all over town, boys
whistle at me – *me*, swinging by in my little pleated skirt, poms in hand.

Day of fervent marigolds. Panties
drying in dormers sway like lily pads
in the benevolent breeze. Don't you see? The whole thing was
a Monet masterpiece. Bits of songs float by –
Saturday Night Fever, the national anthem (that stab of air, that reach
before the final high "thee").

The stadium's a firmament. From the sidelines, the teams charge forth –
we're there, raising our voice in song, some things have
just no sequel.

ADVICE TO ASPIRING SQUAD MEMBERS

You didn't ask for advice, I'm giving it anyway. You think a strong
voice will take you there? Hard thighs? Good palms?

Think again.

You'll need a heart the size of Nunavut. You'll have to be precise in your
affections, yet your sympathies must flex
for today's *rah rah Flames* may be
tomorrow's underdog. The crowds must believe you.

Hidden streams of altruism run within you. Find them, even if it means
renting divining rods. Poms can be affixed to the rods. Open your mind
to anyone who has longed, stood accused, broken through, burned their
villanelles in small, discrete bonfires.

You'll need peerless white sneakers. (In light of this, to cheer

is to bless.) Bless –
        anyone holding their arms
        out to the dark – slicing hoping failing living (Sylvia Plath);

        anyone who, after unsafe
        impolitic sex, loses their head (Ann Boleyn);

        anyone so beautiful, they awake
        as myth &
        blamed for souring the whole story (Pandora).

Ask yourself, do you have what it takes to cheer yourself
out of any box?

IN WHICH I COMPARE MYSELF TO JULIAN OF NORWICH

Julian. Anchoress. All spirit. Attended her own burial (circa 1372).
Her red rain vision, great pellets gushing from a garland, thorns.
His affliction, hers, hearing, it pours
              from inside.

I'm all flesh, bad at goodbyes, always thought Anchorage
a place in Alaska. The times I've fallen
from the world, hands
were there, caught me. Hands.

I starred at my own coronation. Clairol Super Hold my crown.
To give up the world for a box
              to think in, I don't want
to think *that* bad, can't fathom leaving
my *Jane Fonda Workout* videos
behind, my crimson sweater
              heaped at the door.

SPIRIT IN RESIDENCE

I'm not what you think.
I'm no cheap Hallowe'en stunt. No ivory-boned spinster bent, still,
on beating the split infinitives out of them.
No one poisoned me in the garden (so frosh league).
I'm no late oboe Prof who longed to samba (who doesn't hear
a mending music in their head?)

I'm the harpy in the ivy, the caliban-kicker[I]. Even though
dead, I know a fine fall day when
I see one. Look at the girls in their tall new boots. They're
headed for the football field where

with no overhead wires, a mote of late summer
dandelion fluff drifts, out of nowhere, into the defensive
linebacker's retina; in other words

                    if loss *must* mark the day's mythic, otherwise
                    flawless stadium light (*our* loss) –

I'm the sudden gust – the handless blast lifting the crowd –
the last, collective pang: the linger.

[I] She is probably referring, here, to the cheerleading move known as
*aerial: cartwheel without hands touching ground or floor; can also refer to
a walkover or roundoff without hands.* She may be thinking, as well, of
the feisty sprite in the famous Elizabethan bard's late, great comedy,
The Tempest.

TOASTING THE LOWLY, OVERLOOKED COMMA

Here's to you, small sturdy hammock dangling from the inconsequential
twigs of our harangue trees – to you, timber's most restrained cougar
(we dismissed you as tadpole, crooked tear,
curvature of the whine, pit stop on grammar's interstate –
> the kind of place, having tanked up, gets forgotten
> before the coffee's cold).

This is a night for defollyation.
Never were you: moon, spoon. Here's to what you've always known –
many naps make for a great repose amid the rumble, history. You've been
> shafted, short
shrifted as a gaffer with low ambition or
as John Clare wrote Napolean, "the world was on thy page
> of victories, but a comma."

You're bigger than bend
to a means. Booted up the line, made to speak for others – " " –
you're the grapnel that got away, grappling hook we should have loved,
loyal whitecap below our sad little scows. You allow,   , trenchant
delay –

Here's to many more salubrious day trips to MacArthur Park, melting,
anywhere that gives you pause,

CASANOVA QUARTERBACK

You're never too old for love, he says. Remembering my fondness for
melon he tries again. Beneath my balcony, he juggles casaba, honey dew,
bark melon, not fumbling once. Not so different from football,
he calls up, asks if the lady
is pleased. The lady is. I invite my fruity troubadour
in.

He seeks only my ears, calls them exquisite spigots that grow
sweeter with age. He sings *Shiloh* by Neil Diamond. His knife marks
a line on blonde, honeydew skin. He'll not cross this line, he says.
Merely wishes to talk, not jump

my bones. Melon choly bites, he says. He feeds me sucker rain. His face
wears the same rhino skin as the bark melon. We're both tired
of eating alone, woe est
moment in meal. He sings *Baby, We Were Born To Run*.
I'm sure he's been

drinking. Yes, it bites. He should have asked me years ago. Before
he wrecked his knees in the great game of '71. Honey, I say, we're not
eating alone. And I brush a drop of Grecian Formula off the sweet flesh
he holds in his palm.

FINDING MYSELF IN REDUCED CIRCUMSTANCES WITH LITTLE TIME & FEW RESOURCES FOR SAYING GOODBYE

Let me be brief.

Tribe, let me. Let me bleet, beef, be rife. Brief me – bile mile file. Let me
rime. Tremble me, let me feel, rifle free. Fib. Fie. Rib me. Fire me!
Me, bribe? Bet? Belt me. Bib me.
Bite? Beet? Brie melt? Lite beer? Tele me
re: tire rim mire, elm tiers. Lier, lifer,
ire, ebb, brime.
Feel me, felt bit. Be me –

      brieflet, fem, bereft.

III

THE FLAMES

RAZE

The old stadium stands condemned, slated to be torn
down – "safety hazard."

Red leaves swat my bobby socks
as I wander through the worn bleachers,

weave past the long, peeling bench, flask in hand. Only
the odd leak, as I was saying – no need

for a public execution. I've written the mayor a moving
epistle to this effect. I launch my argument

from the team bench, mount air – air declines
to catch me – never mind, nary a drop

lost. The new coliseum will boast a dome, here's to

the bloated egg, the future. How they'll miss
the sky, the fools. No one ever called

the view from the necropolis
bad.

ORIGINAL CHANT *

Heads up! Watch out! The Flames are gonna burn;
Go home – get lost – to ashes you will turn!
Leave the kitchen if you can't stand the heat;
The Flames are really cookin' – their fire can't be beat!

Give me an F, Give me an L, Give me an A, etc.

(Props: faux fire extinguishers, faux hoses, spray crowd
with orange confetti.)

* Copy fight: M.L. Hope, 1973

PRACTICE FOR AN AFTERLIFE (JUST IN CASE)

I will say –

I lived among the pyramids, looked at life
from both sides, now – flier & base. I followed
a noble profession begun at Princeton (home of first
recorded fight song) in 1880. I aspired
to moral fiber & three consecutive handsprings. I never
performed an illegal dismount, never missed
Homecoming or Squad Bonding Retreats, never
wished other squads ill, released
air from their tires or jabbed pins in dolls the image
of their quarterback. I've always been
a team player. Even heaven could zip along better
some days, I'll bet. You could use me for, to quote Tennyson,
better use than fame. OK I know, that case in Texas –
the murdering cheerleader mom – but Texas
gave us all
a bad name. Amen. P.S. I donated my Joni Mitchell LPs
to deserving charities.

THE QUAINT RITUAL OF GETTING THE MAIL WORN THIN

A brindled leaf, caught
in a crosswind
weaves & lights
on my arm reaching
for the box. *Last chance*, the envelope avers. That's what they all say.

The days sing out their lapses. They cost too much.
Free offer, no obligation. *Sure.*

I no longer dab *Charlie* cologne on my wrist before
reaching, hoping the postman might
catch my scent, return
with forgotten glad tidings, greetings from the queen, anything.

I've given up. What can a postal worker say to cheer me?

I no longer set a glowing pumpkin by the mailbox
to attract kids. Fact is, I wish
they'd go away. All those bright fliers never say how to make them
go away.

What can anyone say to cheer me? – There's always another
last chance?

HUM

Hummingbird, you're the ultimate tourist. I hang my coloured lantern
out for you, filled with the kind of margarita
you fancy.

I'm not asking for an extended
debate on Hobbes, just a "how's it goin'?" I don't need reminding
I'm a has-been.

You, world's most compact Harley rider, have no time for
palaver with old bags. You're all rally tilt chug-a-lug burn some
midair rubber, hit
                    & fly.

I'm such a chump. Maybe you never came at all, it was only a gnat
in my ear's lonely boudoir, the drone of some crone dying, somewhere,
the gnaw of brevity.

BIRTHDAY

My geophysics grow fuzzy –
do I live on an island bridged to a mainland or mainly land
trestled to hard
obdurate whereabouts?

This morning, a lamina of frost
on my poms. I brandished it
away, told them it'll be OK because well
because mommy said so (a move sports fans once
called brave front).

But in Optometry, twin words swirl in my orbs –
          pom – poem (variance?)

Where was I?

Thank God for old flames. The aging quarterback
shuffles in (triple bypassed), bearing orchids, video. We share
my chesterfield, wearing our uniforms (faded forms), watch
the great game of '71, his epic touch
down, victory snowing on the end zone & me, there – air
borne, less
          real, even, than now.

THE SINGLE WOMAN'S GUIDE TO SELF-ESTEEM
& SUCCESS IN ANY SOCIAL SPHERE

Repeat after me: I'm no Eleanor Rigby.

Don't dally at the church or anywhere, picking up squashed paper cups
after it's over. All gatherings have a
crack in them, the tiniest hairline fissure only those with finely honed
faculties, card-carrying geniuses such as yourself, can diagnose.
You occupy rare ranks, you who sleuth out the first pangs
of an era in decline, a slow wither the rest of us, with our mole vision
can't see until
it's upon us; you, like oracular seismographers, predict tremblings long
before baby quake has grasped the rudiments of spelling much less learned
its name. The rest of us are mere apologists. Extremists. Too early/too late.
Sorry to rain on the parade but you know how it is, work tomorrow. Or
signals missed entirely. A close friend, whose name I, crossing myself
on the Bible, vowed never to tell, was reported to have dallied for so long
at her host's home, she had to be forcibly removed, was struck from
everyone's lists. Can you blame them? She became
a lonely person. This should be where your keen logic churns into high
gear, splatters a single, resplendent insight across the page – here it is –
my dear friend would have benefited more from a quiet evening at home,
pouring over *Robert's Rules of Order.* I have
often told her so.

Ask yourself: what did Eleanor Rigby do with all that rice?

COCKTAILS AT BRIMSTONE

"When bound and gagged, you can still tap out HELP
in Morse code to attract attention."

from Nancy Drew, *The Clue of the Tapping Heels*

Port Amalgamish College requests the pleasure of trotting you
out once again, Brimstone Hall, RSVP.

I remain vaguely affiliated, allied in some
indeterminate, fobbed off, though not utterly
abandoned way.

Is it:
1. institutional pathos
2. failure to update their mailing list or
3. they like my cream of mushroom casserole?
   I can't tell.

Hell is cocktails at Brimstone. High heels. Name tag:
Hello, my name is Maud-Lynn Hope, Retired Cheerleader
Might as well say *Eleanor Rigby* (all
the lonely people).

If I were Nancy Drew, I could tap my way
out of here. Someone would hear, tell me how
resourceful I am.

Instead, I stand corner-flowered. I sip my way to numbness, believe
only Byron –
        Ah, surely nothing dies
                but something mourns.

EXHIBIT 8A: THE CHEERLEADER AS RELIC [1]

> Even as I grieve, they whittle me in wax –
> breasts hyperbolic, hair – jumbo cartoon yellow. Where did I get those
> cheekbones? I'm Carol Brady[2]-meets-sultry, gorilla-held girl
> in *King Kong*.[3] I'm Nancy Kerrigan[4]-meets-Tonya Harding[5] (sordid little
> tale, that one).

> In another room, an artisan captions me –
> 'Icon: The Enthusiast.'
> Why not dub me
> 'Dream of the Body
>   as Ambivalent Consortium?'

Only my legs look capable of reason.

(I always had good legs.)

.

[1] The curators of the museum realize that, because of her wide array of shifting subject positions combined with her singularly equivocal status within the popular cultural discourses of the time, visitors to the Museum of the Twentieth Century may find the following glosses helpful (they're available, as well, for those taking advantage of our audio tour, on track 8).

[2] Popular television series about a blended family, 1969-1974. Starred Florence Henderson as "Mom" (Carol Brady) & Robert Reed as "Dad" (Mike Brady). The Bradys had a nice home located in California with a brick barbeque in the back yard. Their house has been designated an official historical site.

3 Classic 1933 horror film (dir. Merrian C. Cooper) starred Fay Wray as beauty who tames beast. Frequently remade during the century starring other notable beauties such as Jessica Lange in the 1976 Dino De Laurentis production.

4 Nancy Kerrigan, born Stoneham, Massachusetts, in 1969. Champion figure-skater medallist known for her wholesomeness. Was clubbed in the knee with a metal baton in Detroit during a practice in 1994. The attack was a conspiracy hatched by the ex-husband of Kerrigan's opponent, Tonya Harding, see note, below.

5 Tonya Harding, born Oregon, in 1970. Grew up in a series of trailer parks & other transient homes. At age three, saw skaters at a mall & her destiny flashed before her. Bought skates. Overcame poverty and asthma to rise in the world of professional figure skating. Did her first triple loop at age nine, had nearly perfected the triple axel by her mid-teens. Her tarty, working-class image flew in the face of the chaste, Barbie-aura of the typical figure skater or, as one unidentified source called Tonya, "the pool-playing, drag-racing, trash-talking bad girl of a sport that thrives on illusion." In 1990, married Jeffrey Gillooly who reputedly made a lot of money from the sale of a porn video the two made; these reports remain unconfirmed. Gillooly & his friend, Shawn Eckhardt, three-hundred pound proprietor of World Bodyguard Services, arranged the above-mentioned attack on Nancy Kerrigan in 1994. Harding's already tarnished image suffered greatly & an errant skate-lace hampered her tearful performance in Lillehammer. To date, one of the great figure skating scandals of all time. Surpassed in cheerleading only by the murderous Texas cheerleading mom (no Carol Brady, she!).

THE LONELY PEP QUEEN'S GUIDE TO MARS

I'd like to go far, far away, somewhere over
the wane row, where Jurassic skin marks beauty rare
as a widow's peak or
                greatly prolonged neck.

I'd love to double my fun. The twin moons of Mars
might be the ticket. I've done rustic waterfront weekend. I

need a challenge. The red planet scores high, its lakes
all blown away. I'd like to pack for the weather, throw in some Proust.
Dust storms last for months.

I'd prefer my breath
taken away. Way up high, scaling with my Martian guide
dust-encrusted buttes, ridges, knobs – cherishing

the lightness in my
head (akin to the old victory buzz). I'd like to watch
my back – *we're not at all sure*
who's home – if they insist dry cold's better, agree
& when the moons argue
with each other   *don't take sides.*

SOOTHSAYER

She lived in Don Mills. She had a loose false eyelash but hey, she had a special on leaves. It went like this:

SS (Soothsayer): Why have you come?

MLH (Maud-Lynn Hope, me): I hear things.

SS: Like?

MLH: The sound of one land snapping.

SS: When you're alone in the forest?

MLH: No. Any time.

SS: Your leaves are a mess. You used to leap and twirl. You were admired by many. You were happy. The rest is murk, autumnal Armageddon.

MLH: What does it mean?

SS: You tell me. I'm going to make a fresh pot [leaves, returns].

MLH: Something terrible is going to happen. You just don't want to upset me.

SS: Have you noticed anything unusual?

MLH: Yes. Last night, my dining table, bare. This morning, my Pascal, open, these words highlighted: *We shall die alone.*

SS: Get a new dining table.

TELEPHONE AUDITION FOR THE AFTERLIFE

You there – Cinderette – it's the big squad leader in the sky. I've been watching you &

guess what? Light is political.

Little of your face is
flattered by shadow. & why do you wear training wings, still? –
pretty farm team, if you
ask me. It takes you three hours to watch *Sixty Minutes*. What shall I do with you
meek little spark, peeping pom
on your own kismet? Do you want to spend

eternity milking cows, far from grace?

Didn't anyone say whatever you do, don't ever
ever bore them?

CRIMINALIZATION, IT HAPPENS TO THE BEST OF US

We're driven to it, those small
cheerless springs
do it, that dimness attractive
to thieves. I cruise Cape George in a Subaru
the bank owns. Nothing is mine, that's why the woods owe me
ferns.

The back roads
have back roads – *Rear Settlement, Rear Georgeville* –
Keep out, Private Property
               all signs say.

Some ferns
are sexy, some not. I want hart's tongue, netted chain, ostrich –

Tall zoo of plumes. I haven't felt this
piquant in years (nature's been pixie dust, to me, this
is different) – I dig.

My hostages raise fine lace hackles, bare
whiffs of green. *Do what I say, no one gets hurt* – a line
I'd heard in a gangster flick – (though not *really*
my style).

Suburbia's not so bad
I tell my green victims (though not
precisely true). – Only thing worse than being whacked is being
whacked by a liar, I think, driving to what
passes for home, village of cold
spurning earth.

MAGIC SWEATER

Dear wool amulet, known to ward off evil. I lift it from mothballs,
my old Flames jersey, need it. September & last
night, such a dream – my squad mates & I
under water, essaying
a pyramid in the saddest, deepest lake
known to man, dark, heavy spate toppling
our efforts, no loft. Nor could we swim. We were lost.

I wake wiped out, damp. I tug the lucky
red sweater over my head, sweet noose of roses, reach
for the remote, news. I pull it over stiff
morning joints, my eyes still webbed with dream water.
I'm not seeing things –
                    people fall
from the sky, what new wilderness
                    is this?

The sweater could reverse the tide of history, once. Now it's
mere yarn, it unravels as I watch the screen. As I stand frail, afraid,
red strands rain
onto the floor, off my body, crumbling
cathedral in which
I lived, inclined
          towards belief.

FRANGIBLE

This year, I let everything go, did the unheard of – left
my clay herb pots in the snow, now
they scream splinters. Try to see
the beauty in it, I think. See how
the snow, doming the withered
thatch of oregano
resembles a white derby. Maybe.

Normally, split-pea soup would bubble on my stove, by now.
Normally, I wouldn't use

normally in a poem. Wouldn't try so hard to spot what resembles
something else. The backs of my Adirondack chairs
evoke great white fans. Maybe. That's so

like life, isn't it? – being blessed with fans in a blizzard. I reach
for *Roget's Thesaurus*, another way
to say frail. Frangible. Thank you.

Across the big fence, the president calls his people resilient.

Maybe.

YET ANOTHER BIRTHDAY

Pink balloons tethered to my chair. He pinches my rump
between the slats. Penny for your thoughts, he says (every year

he tells me this; thoughts don't follow the curve
of inflation – they're never worth more).

The *1966 College Football Rulebook* is silent on birthdays, he doesn't
know I only get, poised above the glowing cake, one wish.

You have three wishes, he croons. In earlier days, I might have
set him straight, told him one per birthday.

By this point, I'll take three.

1. I wish the voice in the wilderness would move to town.

2. I wish the orca of dejection that daily eats away at my entrails
    could be slain.

                               (*Wow*, he says)

3. I wish he'd take me to a discotheque.

We both know the discos are gone. We've no clue what people
dance to anymore, or if

they dance. I blow. The room darkens.

STANDARD TIME

One of my lucid days.
        I scan the obits, don't find
        myself. I offer to escort
        myself to the stadium – a lovely
        idea, I say to me. I'm polite
        (though only later
        recall the corsage).

The last hours
        of standard time, I stroll
        through the deserted
        bleachers. Stand where
        Eddie Van Halen stood
        then bend, undo my hair,
        sweep it along home
        team's bench
        rosetted now, with frost.
        This arouses me, what's more

it's safe sex. I can
        think of worse ways
        to spend an hour. *Fall,*
        fall back. What will you do with *your*
        extra sixty minutes? To

know each crevice of
        a place you love is
        a swell thing, the old
        quarterback once said. Claimed
        he knew all of me. He didn't.
        My naval, at its summit
        juts errant, cerise, a rose
        in bud, he whispered.
        It doesn't. Isn't. Wasn't.

FIDELITY

Season's last game. Dirty old day. So few loyal ones
left. I bring ice cream, frigid rain falls. The crusade in mud
goes on, life's great questions disguised
as football. Everyone's home, playing
Wolfenstein while out here, hope still sparks from the sidelines,
the woman in the yellow rain poncho – me.
I alone shout *Go, Flames!* I raise my peanut buster parfait to a distant
faith in something, pull my hood strings
                        until my head resembles a thing caught
happily, in a bag.

MUSING ON NAMES WHILE DRIVING DURING AN OFFICIAL STORM, LISTENING TO JOHNNY CASH, THEN JOAN OSBORNE

A hurricane named Karen. Boy named Sue. Whatever.
What's in a nom de pom? We're just winging it, here.
Mounds of dulse, tangles of purple moppery
dishevel the beach – why not call them cast off
merleader poms? What if the sirens were
us, singing to divert the enemy waterbacks?

The rainy season, someone trying to tell us
something? This road, ricking the brink
of sea (this hobbling path, this blundering trail, this
this, this) renders
dictionaries runnels, sad
gee-tars on stilts, wet despite. The names of things
topple. I'm less sure God's a ravening old man
with void issues; perhaps God's the torrent that humbles
or, as in Joan's tidal wail (cusp)
just a stranger   one of us.

THE AGING CHEERLEADER AS ARSONIST

October. Perfect night for a fire.
For resolve, higher thoughts, compassionate

endings. I consider my beloved
stadium, the wrecking ball's low
blow tomorrow. It racks, dispirits.
I don my old uniform, find matches, go
home, sweet stadium.

A protracted penumbra
has set in. The popcorn sign, having lost
its circus air, hangs all misery-wafted. It's time
to offer the sacred field one last high V, a final set of candlesticks.

Promethe-ette, I strike – flames, tackle-free
tear down the sixty-yard line, dragoon the end
zone where dignitaries sat, fur wrapped – higher, higher –
press box, long poles where hung
lights, it all roars – a toasty ghost-diva sings *God Save Our
Gracious Queen.*

Dear old home, how you burn, you don't disappoint –
Blaze. This
is your ball – most radiant game in town – you earned this
hot night. Out.

THE MORNING NEWS

Last night, while our village slumbered
Amalgamish Stadium was torched. We are saddened
to report that, due to this pre-emptive spark, today's air is laden
with cinder, with ash. We recommend the respiratorially challenged,
victims of asthma & the like
remain inside. The fire is thought
to have begun shortly after midnight, when Chief Shorty McDougall
received the call – "a ring of burning fire" –

"No, no," said Shorty, "that's a Johnny Cash song –
it's love
that's a burning thing." But the caller, un
identified, pressed on – sirens were sent.
Combing the disaster site, college experts
from Combustology recovered
a pom fringe, dated to the Vinyl Era
& a strand of synthetic blonde hair. The lead suspect may be
a female pyromaniac. Secondary suspect –
a Toronto man (Ontario plates
seen here yesterday). No further details have been
released.

"Amalgastead," as it was
lovingly known, was founded in 1881, a joint project
of the Fathers of Funday & the Daughters of Numerous
Grievances. It was designed to promote spiritual fitness
in the days of curfews &
encumbering robes.

> *Says Mayor April McIvor:*
> *"I'm sure we all awake*
> *with drooping hearts; luckily,*
> *the new Mega-Dome is soon*
> *to be assembled, we can get*
> *on with our lives."*

NOTE DISCOVERED BY NONE OTHER THAN YOURSELF

After the fire, I became a recluse.
The fact that you're reading this probably means
I'm dead. I had something grander, if more gothic
in mind, having read "A Rose for Emily" many times.
Alas, our humble town lacks
a degree of ostentation present in the Deep South. Lacks
deep, too (always considered it shallow
little place – I can say that, now). Not to mention my inability to lure
the aging quarterback into my boudoir. Anyway, the streets
have been paved for years. What allowed me
to withdraw from the world was my amazing foresight –
floor to ceiling jello – locker room rainbow –
when the 40-watt bulb smites it at a certain angle, it takes
my breath away. My life has its pattern. Today
for instance, is red. There's a glamour
I never would have supposed, around retreat. Imagine the possibilities
in disappearance. The hush esoteric. If you're reading this &
I'm *not* dead, I expect Oprah's call
any day now.

IV
PROLOGUE

THE AGING CHEERLEADER'S PROLOGUE

Begin by clearing the air.

1. The woman you saw at the highway edge, the disappointed one with the red sweater, the blonde prosthetic ponytail, wasn't me. You must have some other Maud-Lynn Hope in mind.
2. The patient being wheeled through the door marked FACIALS – *far* more big-boned than I am!
3. The witch much taller than the other trick or treaters, likely someone's mom...
4. The dark-glassed beauty fleeing the paparazzi, (sadly), someone else.
5. The famous Farrah-Fawcett-in-pink-bathing-suit poster, crumbled a hundred times then stomped on by eight sumo wrestlers is *not* a dead ringer for me at present!
6. The fan wearing the Dick Nixon mask in the new dome stadium, raising low-score placards after cheerleading stunts & shouting *pitiful kewpie! – you should be ashamed!*, must be a spy from the ECA (Eastern Cheerleading Assoc.).
7. The statuesque knockout waiting, week after week, for the aging quarterback to tear himself from his small, flickering screen & cross town, bearing a rose & some good news, is named Penelope. She's been there a long time. Another heroine. Another story.
8. The Jane Doe led away for tax evasion is capable of infinitely more foul play than yours truly will *ever* be.
9. That is *not* my neuroscan; the inside of my head is *much prettier*.
10. The poster-girl-poet in the vintage vanishing cream ad –
    just some Citizen Vain (some quaint ploy for immortality).

Once you've set the record straight, start fresh. At the end, if
you must.

1. To the college administrators who allowed me to use school letterhead
   even after I allegedly torched the stadium (though this was never
   proven in a court of law), thank you.
1a). Circulation, you too, for letting me keep my borrowing privileges.
2. To my beloved poms, I tried to be a good mother, kept your spirits up,
   your split ends trimmed.
3. To the aging quarterback, don't enter the end zone without me.
4. To you, sports fans, keep on the sunny side. & if they tell you men are
   from Mars, women are from Venus, rejoinder: cheerleaders spring
   from Terra Pindara, the soil of praise.
5. To you, genial ash heap, for warming my aging soles, much obliged.
5a). & you, who endure on the dear, charred earth where once
   the stadium stood,

    look up, see the ragged, red bird,
                    she rises.

ACKNOWLEDGEMENTS

Various events, places, people, and texts inspired this book: the Sage Hill Writing Experience; the "Silence and Conversation" Symposium at St. Peter's Abbey, Saskatchewan; The Leighton Studios at the Banff Centre; the "Art Bar" Reading Series in Toronto; the Chateau Laurier in Ottawa; the Musical Ride; the view of the football field from my office window in Nova Scotia; the autumn of 2001 with all its beauty and heartbreak; Denis De Klerck; Fred Wah, Don McKay; Tim Lilburn; Pier Giorgio Di Cicco; Maria Jacobs. Mary Ellen Hanson's book, *Go! Fight! Win!: Cheerleading in American Culture* (Bowling Green State University Popular Press, 1995), provided useful source material. Barry Lopez's *Arctic Dreams* inspired "I Imagine North." Sina Queyras introduced me to Brenda Shaughnessy's poetry. David Lynes, a former football player from Scarborough, Ontario, has been in my corner, cheering me on for many seasons.

"Finding Myself in Reduced Circumstances with Little Time & Few Resources for Saying Goodbye" is for the Extreme Poets: Donna Kane, Joe Blades, Mary-Louise Rowley, Hillary Clark, Fred Wah.

The tall poems in this book are for Tanis MacDonald.

Thanks to Gillian McCulloch for permission to use her "Crown of Weeds" for cover art, and to Ruth Young and Greg Walsh for their technological prowess.

A somewhat different version of "Criminalization, It Happens to the Best of Us" was published in the anthology, *Coastlines: The Poetry of Atlantic Canada* (Goose Lane Editions, 2002); thanks to the editors.

Jeanette Lynes' previous two collections of poetry are
A Woman Alone on the Atikokan Highway and *Left Fields*,
both published by Wolsak and Wynn. She received the
Bliss Carman Poetry Award in 2001, and her poems are
frequently broadcast on CBC Radio.

Jeanette teaches at St. Francis Xavier University
and works as an associate editor
at *The Antigonish Review*.